30 DAYS OF DREAMS AND VISIONS

"For Thirty Days I Am Going to Give You Dreams and Visions. Proclaim My Words!" God

ALLYSSA NARVAEZ

ISBN: 0692391258
ISBN 13: 9780692391259
Library of Congress Control Number: 2015902911
Harold Publishers, Lansing, MI

GRATITUDE

Gratitude is a word that expresses our thankfulness to ones who have labored for us to achieve visions. I express my gratitude to Christ; The Holy Spirit for revealing these visions and bringing me these dreams. I want to thank him for choosing me as a vessel to "proclaim his words" in a world that may not receive his advice, warnings and even his grace. I want to thank The Holy Spirit for the office of Prophecy. I dedicate this Book to Salvation.

I want to thank my parents Barbara and Tom Cummins who have labored with me. I would like to thank my children for enduring challenges of church leadership. I would like to thank spiritual leaders, friends and family that gave words of encouragement along the way.

TABLE OF CONTENTS

INTRODUCTION

What world do we live in today? This is the year of the proclamation of Jesus Christ as our Lord and Savior. I will tell you what world we live in. We live in a world that is fast decaying to the grips of the enemy. We live in a world where the enemy wants all people to believe a lie; the lie that Salvation is not a complete necessity to inherit eternal salvation in the Kingdom of Paradise.

The pages in this book bring truth, reality and hope for the non-believer. They bring a call to the ones with inherited salvation already. These pages birth out The Office of An Evangelist; which is what Christ Commissions us to do. We are charged to take the full armor of GOD into the harvest and gather the grapes for his vineyard.

II Timothy 4:5 But watch thou in all things, endure afflictions, do the work of an evangelist, make full proof of thy ministry. (KJV)

Mathew 21:33-43 Hear another parable: 'There was a certain household-er, which planted a vineyard, and hedged it round about, and digged a winepress in it, and built a tower, and let it out to husbandmen, and went into a far country: And when the time of the fruit drew near, he sent his servants to the husbandmen, that they might receive the fruits of it. And the husbandmen took his servants, and beat one, and killed another, and stoned another again, he sent other servants more than the first: and they did unto them likewise. But last of all he sent unto them his son, saying, they will reverence my son. But when the husbandmen saw the son, they said among themselves, This is the heir; come, let us kill him, and let us seize on his inheritance. And they caught him, and cast him out of the vineyard, and slew him.

When the lord therefore of the vineyard cometh, what will he do unto those husbandmen?

They say unto him, He will miserably destroy those wicked men, and will let out his vineyard unto other husbandmen, which shall render him the fruits in their seasons. Jesus saith unto them, Did ye never read in the scriptures, The stone which the builders rejected, the same is become the head of the corner: this is the Lord's doing, and it is marvellous in our eyes?

Therefore say I unto you, The kingdom of GOD shall be taken from you, and given to a Nation bringing forth the fruits thereof." (KJV)

Christ is coming back someday and he will look for those who have gathered the fields.

Will you be one, who he can say, he is well pleased. Will you be ready to give account of your office of an evangelist?

Mathew 25:21 His lord said unto him, Well done, thou good and faithful servant: thou hast been faithful over a few things, I will make thee ruler over many things: enter thou into the joy of thy lord (KJV)

Reward in Heaven

DAY 1
Tuesday
January 21, 2014
REWARD IN HEAVEN

Jesus is in the Middle of Everything! Leading and guiding us. People of God I dreamed; I tried to go through an unfamiliar door in relative's house. The door was different. When I pushed the door there was resistance; before I could open the door, the largest thump can from the other side of the door. I instantly felt The Holy Spirit telling me don't go through that door. The Holy Spirit spoke to me, "This is serious Nikki; you are earning your credit in heaven. Follow my spirit, wait on me."

We can not afford to take the wrong paths! It is effecting our graduation to new blessings; even in eternity. Those that wait on The Lord will be rewarded with purpose and destiny. God has great plans for you. Mathew 16:27 For the Son of man shall come in the glory of his Father with his angels; and then he shall reward every man according to his works.

My Family calls me Nikki and so does the Holy Spirit, but sometimes he changes from calling me Nikki and calls me different names and titles. God told me while church planting outside of Nashville, Tennessee, "When Satan tries to catch you in the Spirit World; I have already changed your name. I'm two steps ahead of him." Satan is chasing the old me and I have already transposed into a new anointing. God's sovereign plan makes me thing of:

> Isaiah 54:17 No weapon that is formed against thee shall prosper; and every tongue that shall rise against thee in judgment thou shalt condemn. This is the heritage of the servants of the LORD, and their righteousness is of me, saith the LORD. (KJV)

No weapon Satan fires will prosper but, they will come into the obedience of Christ. This is why we can rejoice in The Midst of The Battle!

The Spirit of Distraction

DAY 2
Wednesday
January 22, 2014
THE SPIRIT OF DISTRACTION

I dreamt My Uncle Richard asked me to watch his horse while he was away for a couple days. My uncle is a lover or horses. We would often visit his farm in Covert, Michigan as children. His farm had chickens, pigs and plenty of horses. A great escape for a city girl as myself. I dreamt I rode the horse and when we returned to the stable the horse drank his water in a lying position. A horse doesn't usually lie down. I thought the horse didn't look well. He was sick. In my dream I was headed in the car to see my Uncle. An unknown woman was driving the car. I was on the cell phone speaking to him and telling him about his horse. As I was talking, this woman was driving and talking. I mean she just chattered. She would go up in pitch and down in her pitch. She reminded me of blah!.....blah!..... blah!..... blah! In an irritating way and she was distracting me from my conversation with my Uncle Richard. I exhaled! "Will You Please Be Quiet! I am trying to talk to my Uncle about his horse!"

Instantly she missed the curve. The car was supposed to make the bend. We missed the bend. We were headed directly into the lake. The lake reminded me of the small side lakes by a viaduct, small enough to conqueror if you are an

3

excellent swimmer, but large enough to drown if the Lord doesn't rescue you. At that moment my spiritual man could sense, she jerked the wheel into the direction of the lake. She did it on purpose! My physical being said to my Uncle on the phone, "She has driven us into the lake, Oh Jesus!" I opened the door swiftly. I looked in the back seat while thinking to myself, "Ok I can make this. The lake is not that bad. I can swim." In the back seat I saw my 4 year old daughter Kennedy. She had come along for the ride. She instantly started unbuckling her seat belt as I told her "Kennedy come to mommy we are going into the lake but mommy is going to save you", she kept saying, "No! No! I'm scared." "Kennedy listen to me!" I demanded. Come to the front with mommy as I had one hand on the door and the other grabbing for my baby. I could feel the woman's thoughts as she said, "Oh, I'm going make it."

As I awoke the Lord said, "This dream has a meaning", and I thought, "Why how could a nightmare like that have a meaning?" The Holy Spirit said, "Let's go over it. "Ok Lord" I replied, "Who was in the car with you?" The Holy Spirit asked, I replied, "A woman." The Holy Spirit Replied, "Yes that was The Spirit of Distraction." I instantly got the revelation in my soul and I thought to myself, "Yes, she was distracting me from the conversation by going on and on. She knew I was preoccupied a telephone conversation. The Lord replied, "She took you off course, and whenever The Spirit of Distraction takes you off course, it places you right in the middle of harms danger." I also knew and recognized the moment I acknowledged her she retaliated with taking the car into the water. The "Spirit of Retaliation" was the main Pig in the Parlor. This is why it is imperative to counteract the spirit of retaliation with a prayer of covering for ourselves, children and loved ones. The enemy can attack our anointing through the doors we leave open and unattended.

I thought to myself, "Why was The Woman: The Spirit of Distraction driving? Why did she have the wheel in the first place? Never give the foul Spirit of Distraction the wheel. We can prevent this by being obedient to the voice of God.

The day prior to this dream, I received and invitation to Minister in Abuja, Nigeria Africa. I was considering the invitation until a trusted advisor told me of how the violence is rampant there with militia. The enemy will try and distract you with God's own will. God spoke to me clearly in the night of Wednesday January 22, 2014. He said, "I am going to give you 30days of Dreams and Vision. Proclaim my words."

DESIRES OF THE HEART

DAY 3
Thursday
January 23, 2014
DESIRES OF THE HEART

I dreamed again on the third day. I thought, Ok this is real! Everything about God is real. Everything about our lives is real and from Christ. The Bible reads in Isaiah:

> Isaiah 43:7 Even every one that is called by my name: for I have created him for my glory, I have formed him; yea, I have made him. (KJV)

In my dream on this night I was a Pastor to a very large congregation. The congregation was my nationality; I had a connection with the people spiritually. In the dream I needed to take a trip somewhere and I left for a few days. In my dream I was unaware if I left for business, ministry or vacation, but I needed to fly out of town for just a few days. I returned to the city days later. When I attended church, I found there was another woman who was walking into the Pulpit wearing a clergy robe. She had a distinguished aura about herself. She was the new Pastor. I went to walk up to the pulpit but I was no longer recognized as The Leader of the house. I had on regular clothing and I did not wear a robe in the dream. She began to shake everyone's hand in the pulpit in an introductory

8

"Welcome to My House Style." When the Minister of the Service introduced The Speaker, she stepped up and walked pass and over me into the podium. I was not delivering The Word of GOD! I could not believe it. The church had changed. The church was no longer the soul stirring fire brewing Holy Ghost filled House of GOD, but it was still, refined and a different nationality of people.

Thus sayeth The Spirit of God, "The heavens have shifted and we are in a new style of worship but the Church of Christ; Gods people are behind the times. The Spirit World has shifted and left the best Preachers behind because their hearts have left for vacations, business meetings and five-star resort style sinning. We must come back to a place of true worship because this is The Final Call. Restore your position in me and my kingdom. You have one last chance to get it right!"

Rev 2:4-5 Nevertheless I have somewhat against thee, because thou hast left thy first love. Remember therefore from whence thou art fallen, and repent, and do the first works; or else I will come unto thee quickly, and will remove thy candlestick out of his place, except thou repent. (KJV)

Rev 3:1 And unto the angel of the church in Sardis write; These things saith he that hath the seven Spirits of God, and the seven stars; I know thy works, that thou hast a name that thou livest, and art dead. (KJV)

KINGDOM ASSIGNMENTS

DAY 4
Friday
January 24, 2014
KINGDOM ASSIGNMENTS

The Holy Spirit said, "I want you to go to sleep by 9:00p.m. because, I am going to appear to you." I replied. "Yes Lord." Every night I raced to get in the bed and go to sleep. I was eager to know the next dream. To feel the Holy Spirit in my dreams is simply breathtaking. When you awake from the dream you find yourself swept-up in The Spirit of God. His glory simply fills the room.

I dreamed I was on a beach. I was in a young adult. I was old enough to work because I had a job at the local beach store ran by an Oriental Woman. I was playing with her grand-daughter.

"Come on! Let's go swimming! She Exclaimed. "I can't. I have to go to work." I replied. She pulled me by the arm. "Oh come on! It will be fun. My grandmother won't mind. You're with me" She said. The young girl didn't have a name in the dream. "Well ok, I guess one swim will not hurt." I thought while smiling. We joined the other teens on the beach. They were playing race in the water. Whoever got to a certain point in the water and made it back to shore won the game.

I found a good spot on the right of the beach. The left seemed to be dirty. The other children didn't really seem to mind. Someone shouted! Get Ready! Get Set! Go! The kids dove in the water and began racing. Then suddenly we saw a large fish and I thought, "it's a whale or something" until I looked further and saw two fins on its back. It was a shark! Some kids in the race seemed not to see the shark because they were still racing. I could see three kids that were cheerers in my right peripheral vision on the beach shore. We all began to scream Shark! Shark! Shark! But they could not hear us. There was one of my school aged best friends swimming in the water. "Ladonn! Ladonn! Come back." I began to call. We were the best of friends growing up. In my dream while she was in the water, she was and experienced swimmer. Her shapely body glided in and out of the water like a professional. I was hollering to her "L.a.d.o.n.n !! Come back there is a shark!" We were all hysterical! The swimmers realized we were screaming Danger! Danger! They saw the shark! For a split second the shark was contemplating who to go after, Ladonn on the left or the other kids on the right. As they began to turn to shore to swim to safety the shark chose my friend Ladonn. My heart sank! There was no preference as to who the shark selected. I think it was luck of the draw. I hated to see him choose the one I knew and loved. Why couldn't he select someone else? I thought in the dream.

She began swimming! I thought, "She has it. She is going to get away. She's going to make It." but the shark was just too fast. First he bit off her foot and ankle with one bite. Then within three bites he had consumed her body all except her head which seemed to ascend on top of the sharks head. It was as her body lay under the shark's exterior layer of skin instead of in his stomach but he had eaten her. You could see her body's silhouette but her head was exposed. I could see the pain in her eyes. The pain of knowing he had captured her. "Throw me a knife" I shouted to someone. I was going to cut her out! She and the shark were now sitting on the shore. She was still inside his body. The shark could sit up; it could breathe outside the water! Satan takes on many different forms, transforming himself into an angel of light, deceiving even the very elect of God if it were possible. I could see my friend clenching both her fist and clinching her eyes shut back and forth. She was expressing death and the fact that she had lost the battle all at the same time. She had lost at living. She lost at seeing her life and her children's lives. She had lost at her chance of eternity in Paradise. She gurgled.… S.A.V.E.….. M.E.….. N.I.K.K.I.!

I went to run toward to her to cut her out. I screamed, "Call on Jesus Ladonn!!!" with sheer terror for her in my heart. She gurgled as her body was consumed and began decomposing J-E-S-U.… She couldn't even get the whole name out! As he consumed her; in the spirit I could feel; she was transforming and transferring into his spirit; the adversary.

Romans 10:13 For whosoever shall call upon the name of the Lord shall be saved. (KJV)

I stopped "Wait! I can't cut her out or it will eat me" I thought to myself. I couldn't even save her. She was gone. I was so sorry! Eaten by Satan, devoured and couldn't get the name Jesus out! My question to you is: what about those who have not or can't call on the name of Jesus. They just don't have time on their side. They don't have the strength. Save the ones you love before its simple too late!

I awoke feeling like my heart was in my throat. "These are nightmares" I said. The Holy Spirit Replied, "No, these are not nightmares but they are Revelations."

Thus sayeth The Spirit of God to you, "I am a consuming fire. I present myself the way I desire. I make myself into a dream of warning. I make myself into a sweet dream of lilies and marigolds. I can make myself come into your dreams, but a dream is a picture of what's to come. This is the final call. Gather my grapes for the processing. The time is here. I am looking for ripe grapes for only the best will do. The prophet has spoken. Where is your bushel to bring to the groomsmen wedding? Gather my barn. Evangelize." The Am That I Am.

As I saw a vision of people with bushels of grapes on their shoulder strap saying, "I have my grapes" Another said, "I have my grapes."

Isaiah17: 5-7 And it shall be as when the harvestman gathereth the corn, and reapeth the ears with his arm; and it shall be as he that gathereth ears in the valley of Rephaim. Yet gleaning grapes shall be left in it, as the shaking of an olive tree, two or three berries in the top of the uppermost bough, four or five in the outmost fruitful branches thereof, saith the Lord GOD of Israel. At that day shall a man look to his Maker, and his eyes shall have respect to the Holy One of Israel. (KJV)

SAME NIGHT A DIFFERENT SONG

DAY 5
Saturday
January 25, 2014, 3:00am
SAME NIGHT A DIFFERENT SONG

This is a voice that was played of the Trumpet to me about the book of Ezekiel. The Holy Spirit said to me while in prayer, "Hear the voice of The Lord. Ezekiel was used as a sign. Go to Ezekiel 12." I replied, "Yes Lord." I began reading and when I got to the fourth verse, my spirit quickened and when read to the seventh verse the Holy Spirit told me to stop! It read:

> Ezekiel 12:4-7 Then shalt thou bring forth thy stuff by day in their sight, as stuff for removing: and thou shalt go forth at even in their sight, as they that go forth into captivity. Dig thou through the wall in their sight, and carry out thereby. In their sight shalt thou bear it upon thy shoulders, and carry it forth in the twilight: thou shalt cover thy face, that thou see not the ground: for I have set thee for a sign unto the house of Israel. And I did so as I was commanded: I brought forth my stuff by day, as stuff for captivity, and in the even I digged through the wall with mine hand; I brought it forth in the twilight, and I bare it upon my shoulder in their sight. (KJV)

The Holy Spirit continued to speak, "So are you being used as an example to many nations. The different nationalities in your dreams represent your exposure to many nations. Use what you have in you hands like Ezekiel to dig your way through, not out but through. You have a pen and a light in your hand right now (I was holding the cell phone for the use of the light to write in the dark.) I am The Light and the pen is My Voice. Proclaim my words. This is your portal to the entrance of the hearts and minds of the people nationally. Get ready to minister, preach, pray, deliver and set the captives free. In less than 30 days, stay focused. Use the light and your hand. I am with you. Selah"

Does God speak to you?

God speaks for he says in the Psalms, if we will be sensitive to hear his voice. Psalms 95:7 For he is our GOD; and we are the people of his pasture, and the sheep of his hand. Today if ye will hear his voice. (KJV)

God speaks to those whom he knows.

John 10:3 To him the porter openeth; and the sheep hear his voice: and he calleth his own sheep by name, and leadeth them out. (KJV)

Do you obey what you hear from God?

John 10:27 My sheep hear my voice, and I know them, and they follow me: (KJV)

If you are challenged with hearing the voice of God, put the book down and ask God to give you clarity with hearing, discerning and knowing his voice and to give you the braveness to follow his commands.

The Hand

DAY 5
Saturday
January 25, 2014
THE HAND

I dreamed I was with my mother Barbara and a cousin Courtney. My cousin asked me, "Will you give us pedicures?" I said, "Sure! That will be fun." I thought to myself that it will be fun for us girls to have girlie treatments and spend time together. My mother then said, "Nikki, I need you to pull these nails out of my hands. They are getting so bad I can hardly move my hands." I replied, "Ok." I looked at my mother's hands; they were full of slender silver hammering nails. The type of nails, you would use to build things. The sharp tips stuck out like splinters. I began to pull the nails out, starting with the round head of the nails. The nails were long and sharp. I told her, "Brace yourself; this one is going to be painful." I collected at least 30 nails from each hand, but the anticipated pain did not seem to affect my mother so much. The way she spoke about the need of them being removed "again" made me know the nails in her hands were a reoccurring thing. It was inevitable, within a matter of time the nails would reappear and become so annoying, they would need to be removed again.

Thus sayeth The Spirit of GOD, "The hand represents The Body of Christ. The nails represent the afflictions of the righteous are many but The Lord delivers them all. Your deliverance is based on the amount of nails you can bear. My Son bear two in his hands and he was delivered into the priesthood. Your nails are smaller but many, as your afflictions are smaller. I am GOD and I can handle many. I know you are able to bear this cup. Jehovah Jireh Your Provider."

WHERE DO I BELONG?

DAY 6
Sunday
January 26, 2014
WHERE DO I BELONG?

I dreamed I was in the FBI or possibly the CIA. I believe I was in one of these organizations because my dream took place in a covert operation; in a highly controlled and secure facility. I was outside the building and engaged right in the line of fire. I was a new recruit or maybe in a witness protection program. I was being protected. "Stand behind me." The Agent demanded as we stood on the fine line between the criminal and the open gun fire. We were on a sidewalk next to the opening of the secure facility. We were using the corner of the building for cover. The Agent was protecting me from the gunfire. The scenario reminded me of a high action movie. She had a shortened shot gun, the military black style with a pump. The criminal had the same type of weaponry. He fired his shortened riffle and the agent was hit. I could have been shot, but The Agent purposely stood in the way of the bullet in order to save me. I picked up the riffle and ran into the "The Secure Facility."

As I walked in I couldn't help but notice the cleanliness of "The Agency." The building was clean and it had nice furniture. The architectural design were straight lines, and very modern. There were rolls of steel on the floor as you would see at a construction site. Maybe they were building high tech weapons or maybe they were preparing for satellite weaponry. The environment was chaotic. I am sure we were in a war. There was bomb fire outside and helicopters everywhere. Inside this "Agency Building" people were working quietly. Every room I passed I saw men wearing white lab coats which made me believe they were scientists, and engineers. They were working in groups. I even saw soldiers wearing blue and white military duty uniforms, placing you in the mind of mall security. They did not wear the modern military uniforms in army green. Their uniforms were blue and white. Their uniforms represented the blue and white that governments wear. They were colors of governmental wars.

Then a short Black Woman approached me. She had a large mouth. She was wearing deep mulberry colored lip stick. The largeness of her mouth seemed to represent authority. She was wearing an all white decontamination suit. "What are you doing in here?" She asked. "I.....I..." before I could reply. She stated firmly! "You don't belong over here" "I do!" I replied. She looked at me suspiciously. "Oh really, who is your Commanding Officer?" She questioned me in a mocking tone with a look that said, "You are caught and you know you are caught and not to mention; you have been exposed." I knew I was in a top secret area but I knew; I also belonged there! I responded to her, "My commanding officer is a Black Woman, I forgot her name." I had not been on the team long and simply forgot. I knew I belonged there simply because of the Agent that just died for me outside by protecting me from the bullets! I belonged here! I stood my ground. I knew I couldn't go outside, there was war out there. She demanded, "You belong on the other side! Come on lets go!" As I followed the woman who was escorting me to "The Other side" She stated obviously, "You can't get a man on this side. You know "your" man has to come from over there." She was insinuating, I wasn't good enough for the nice men on her side, the men that wore blue and white uniforms and lab coats, but I only deserved the "Other Side".

We were walking and she was leading. She called loudly, "Jimmy! "Lift the gate." She stated. I was lead into a work area of Jimmy and his other crew members. It was greasy and dirty in there. It was as if this area was the final stop before reaching the other side. Jimmy and his crew painted the picture of a large black men, bountiful in muscles wearing a leather apron. Jimmy had an iron of some sort in one hand and used the other hand to touch button that lifted the gate. Maybe he was a blacksmith. Blacksmiths are known to make weapons. It was clear he was in the middle of something, making weapons possibly, but he took the time to stop and follow her instructions. As I walked through Jimmy's work area which was dim but gave a little light due to the hanging, metal circular, light fixture in the middle of the room. She escorted me to the "other side".

When I walked into the other side, the people were very, very poor. There was pestilence and disease everywhere. Poverty was everywhere. Not only financial poverty but the sadness of the heart type of poverty, due to the conditions they were living in. There was no joy. I could literally feel the Spirit of Depression in the air. I could feel the Spirit of Loneliness. I could feel the Spirit of Heartache and Disappointment. I could smell the sadness just like you can smell then rain. You don't see rain but you know it isn't far away. Disparity was there! "How could I belong on this side?" I thought and questioned to myself. I awoke with my heart quenched.

Thus sayeth the Spirit of The True and Living God, "We are in Armageddon right now ladies and gentlemen. We do not realize where we belong ourselves. We look to other people to tell us where we, my children belong. You belong on the side where the grass is not greener but always green. You belong on the side of my glory. You belong on the side of truth. You belong on the side of healing. You belong on the side of grace. You belong on the Grand Finale of When the Saints go Marching In. You belong to me! Selah."

I am reminded of doubt and condemnation. The Lord says in, "Galatians 5:1 Stand fast therefore in the liberty wherewith Christ hath made us free, and be not entangled again with the yoke of bondage." (KJV)

You Are Free!

"Rom 8:1 There is therefore now no condemnation to them which are in Christ Jesus, who walk not after the flesh, but after the Spirit." (KJV)

You Are Free! You Are Free! You Are Free!

The war of the flesh vs. spirit and the devil, desires to keep us, in our pasts and our yesterdays but God is clearly telling us to come out of self-doubt. We are thinking we are not good enough. We are listening and believing people such as the woman who seemed to have authority. I was listening to her as she kept telling me in my dream "I did not belong over there". You can identify the people, who say, act and demean our existence in "The Light". God says we are Kings and Priests. Rev 1:6 (KJV). We must liberate ourselves and know, walk and perform like we belong to God!

Who is at Your Door?

DAY 7
Monday
January 27, 2014
WHO IS AT YOUR DOOR?

I dreamt some one was at my parent's front door. They bammed on the door vehemently. I went to the door. It was a man tall and dazed looking. He looked as though he was in the height of a crazed drug addiction and needed to get higher.

"Let me in" He demanded. I looked at him more intensely to see if I recognized him. I did not recognize him. He was not a familiar face. I thought to my self, "I am not letting you in here!"

I went to my step-father Tom who was asleep on the couch. "Tom wake-up!" "Tom! Wake up!" My step-father Tom stands 6'3 and weights at least 220 pounds. He has retired with a Lumber Business. He is a lumber jack and big. I thought by waking Tom I would have re-enforcement. Tom loves to sleep and he was dead asleep and he would not wake up. While I am trying to wake Tom this man goes to the full sized sliding glass patio window that sits in the front of my parent's home. He starts to look wildly through the window. He can't see me because I am bending down trying to wake up TOM! The man screams like a wild beast continuously, "Let Me In." and I awake from this dream.

Thus sayeth The Spirit of GOD. "Listen to the voice of the man. It is a voice of despair. It is a voice of the wild man in the jungle cutting him self and crazed. This is the sound of the woman crying to open the Sheppard's door. This is the sound of the child screaming for my love. This is the sound of you at the point of destruction and this is the sound of my love. Man can not open the door but only The Shepherd. I am The Sheppard and if any many knock, I open the door. Any man means, any state of a man. Look for the ones that need the door to be opened. You have been commissioned. Commissioned means to become assigned to a job, with full benefits and commitment. My pay is high and my rewards are mighty. Don't stand in the way of the door but step aside. I am the one that heals the "vehemently" with grace. I am The Lord of Life and the strength of all salvation, those that trust in me how can they fear. Step inside where the coffee is hot and the fire is warm. Step into my love that fights the battle for you. Step into Salvation."

I am speechless and full of praise, worship and God's love. I have no words to say. If given a social media interface I would tweet #totallyunanticipated

Rent is Due

DAY 8
Tuesday
January 28, 2014
RENT IS DUE

I went to the Thrift Store. The store sold hardware items and fixed broken things. If it was broken they could likely fix it. They were a fix it store. I needed an item that cleaned up the tree shavings after you would cut the tree down. My step-father owned a Tree Business and I often helped him so I was familiar with the business of tree removal. I entered the local owned small shop. They sold repaired furniture also. I entered and saw a tall slender white man. He was accompanied with a female store clerk. I believe they were married and ran the shop as living together. The man said, "Hello Ma'am can I help you?" It felt was as if he knew I was coming or was expected me. I had the notion the item was reserved just for me. In the Prophet's dreams there are some things that are not spoken by God but you just know in your spirit. You are revealed the mysteries. It is not an intuition but a mystery unveiled by The Holy Spirit in you.

I replied, "Yes I need to rent a device that will clean up tree clippings. "Yes we have just what you need." The man stated. The woman took me to a device that had a hose with a vacuum on the end, the canister styled. The canister style device had clearly been rented a bit and used. It exhibited hues of paint missing and some scratch marks. I dreamt the woman held the handle up to show me the item and I asked, "How much does it cost to rent?" She gave me a price. It was pricy was too pricy for me. Immediately I knew I could not afford it. There was no possibly was this item was in my budget. I inquired further for the price. "Does it turn your clippings into a door once your processed the clippings?" She said yes and the price changes every time you process a door. Once you process a door the price automatically increases and you continue to process doors ever so often and you cash out at the end of every week. In essence the true price is not revealed until you use the product repeatedly. When it was time to cash out you simply stop in the store and paid the bill. The device had the capability to communicate your usage with the store. This device would clearly do the work for me but I simply could not afford it. Have you ever went into a store, car store, furniture store, clothing store or any type of store selling an item you wanted, but you simply did not have the money the seller required to received the item? This is how I felt discouraged, annoyed and hopeless. "I can't afford it" I stated. When I said I could not afford it the woman began to walk away with a total lack of interest. The man came from behind the work counter. "Well just a minute young lady. He gestured. I think I may be able to help you." He continued as the woman looked on perturbed. "I can give you this item you so desperately need but it will be only given based on your faith. Your faith can purchase it for you." I replied with surprising eyes, "I will be willing to accept that." The woman was clearly agitated. I can imagine she was thinking. "How can faith pay our bills?" I asked, "You mean to tell me I can have this item as long as I give faith?" He replied "Yes! I also have the faith that eventually one day you will come back and pay for it. You can have it but only if you purchase it with your faith." He stated. I then awoke.

Thus sayeth The Holy Spirit. "We are in a time where there are machines to do the work but we must apply faith because we all know that faith with out works is dead. The dead things in your life are always activated in the Spirit

Realm by your faith. Everyone I healed was based on their faith they could be healed. Every request you have with me is dependant on your faith to receive what is not seen. To walk by faith you must activate assurance; the blessed assurance that I am yours and you are mine. Believe in me is all I require."

BONUS ROUND #1

God said, "The bonus round is a round in life where I pour out my extra spirit prophesied by the prophet Isaiah. The Bonus Spirit is the Spirit of the Seven Spirits of God. I have given the keys of the kingdom to those that follow my lines in the play script and at the end and do not forget their parts. I give them the seven keys to the bonus spirit when they are at full capacity of the latter rain. The latter rain is your ability to receive that which the prophet Isaiah told you about: The Seven Spirits of God. Stay with me it is a rather easy process.

1. Deny the flesh
2. Deny yourself
3. Deny the adversary quickly
4. Believe in me
5. Trust in Me
6. Never give up hope because without hope your patience will fail and finally, believe in Christ, My Son who died not only for you but the Muslim too.

Discrimination of My Spirit to the non-believer is the new wave of the adversary. Salvation was not only for the Jews but the Gentiles also. Take the office of an evangelist and I have delivered the seven keys to the kingdom in your hands. My Spirit has spoken."

Isaiah 64:12 Wilt thou refrain thyself for these things, O Lord? wilt thou hold thy peace, and afflict us very sore? (KJV)

Isaiah 38:16 O Lord, by these things men live, and in all these things is the life of my spirit: so wilt thou recover me, and make me to live. (KJV)

The Seven Spirits of God:

Isaiah 11:2 And the spirit of the LORD shall rest upon him, the spirit of wisdom and understanding, the spirit of counsel and might, the spirit of knowledge and of the fear of the LORD; (KJV)

Keys of The Kingdom:

Revelations 3:1 And unto the angel of the church in Sardis write; These things saith he that hath the Seven Spirits of GOD, and the seven stars; I know thy works, that thou hast a name that thou livest, and art dead. (KJV)

Mat 16:19 And I will give unto thee the keys of the kingdom of heaven: and whatsoever thou shalt bind on earth shall be bound in heaven: and whatsoever thou shalt loose on earth shall be loosed in heaven.

Mathew 16:14-20 And they said, Some say that thou art John the Baptist: some, Elias; and others, Jeremias, or one of the prophets. He saith unto them, But whom say ye that I am? And Simon Peter answered and said, Thou art the Christ, the Son of the living GOD. And Jesus answered and said unto him, Blessed art thou, Simon Barjona: for flesh and blood hath not revealed it unto thee, but my Father which is in heaven. And I say also unto thee, That thou art Peter, and upon this rock I will build my church; and the gates of hell shall not prevail against it. And I will give unto thee the keys of the kingdom of heaven: and whatsoever thou shalt bind on earth shall be bound in heaven: and whatsoever thou shalt loose on earth shall be loosed in heaven. Then charged he his disciples that they should tell no man that he was Jesus the Christ. (KJV)

PROPHECY

DAY 9
Wednesday
January 29, 2014
PROPHECY

Thus sayeth GOD, "I want you to write about The Potter. Tell my people The Potter makes clay and in-order to get the item he desires; he has to mold the clay. Now we all know I am The Potter and they are the clay. The clay doesn't ask, demand or suggest the item he desires to be. The clay gets on the wheel and is spun. Just as I spun you out of the last trial I am spinning you through this trial; not out but through. The difference between out and through are the results. With out you get relief and gold; but with through you get a finished product that is worth more than gold. The treasures I offer are far better then gold, diamonds pearls and rubies because my treasures are a life time of happiness, peace, serenity and purpose. You can't get purpose through a magazine; you don't call up and send your mail order in but purpose comes from being an instrument ready to be played by the trumpeters. I blow the horns and sound the alarms. Are you willing to be used by me? Are you ready to be groomed by me? Are you available to be blown by me? Music is the sound of love. It is a sound I gave to you for the purpose of praising me and The Angels are standing by waiting to help you blow your horns. With every blow releases a little part of your purpose; but you must wrap your lips around the stem in order to feel the sound of purpose. Selah

CHOSEN

DAY 10
Thursday
January 30, 2014
CHOSSEN

I dreamt I was in a mattress store and my family and I were purchasing mattresses. The mattress store was located inside a mall. The process of buying mattresses was very long. This mall seemed to be a place where everyone that knew each other gathered for hellos and laughter. I laid my body on the mattresses; trying them out. Awe this one feels nice. I went to another mattress; awe this one feels better. I walked around a bit. I watched all the people in the mall as they walked by. There was something unusual to me about the people in the mall. I could literally see their challenges with sin. I could see there lusts, desires and short comings. There were a group of men gathering with laughter and say to one another, "how have you been; it has been a while." They reminded me of men at the Super bowl pre-party. They were sharply dressed men. Ever so often I would catch one or two glance at me with admiration. There was one distinctly dressed man. He stood out from the rest. He began walking towards me. He was very handsome. He was about mid- height with wavy cold black hair. His hair shined bright like a pearl with silhouettes and hues of brilliant radiance. He looked as though he was partially Black, with Spanish and German descents. He wore a large and beautiful diamond cross around his neck and glistening diamond bracelet. He flaunted a diamond watch on is wrist. He wore pinkie diamond rings which were breathtaking. He wore all diamonds. The jewelry was very attractive and he seemed to sparkle when he approached me. He talked swiftly and was definitely the chooser, and I was being chosen. When he got in front of me he asked,

"Hey Lady how are you?' I could hear the Holy Spirit telling me to "Stand Up". I began to rise up from under my brother's arm. My brother and I were sitting on a couch waiting for our purchases to be completed. My brother George is a beautiful man. He has grace, patience and is a man of high morals.

The Holy Spirit was preparing me to witness to this fancy man as he told me to stand to my feet. As I prepared in my mind to witness to this man about Christ, that small still voice that says "get ready they are coming, tell them about John 3:16 my love. " For God so loved the world that he gave his only begotten Son, that whosoever believeth in him should not perish, but have everlasting life" (KJV). I replied gently to the man as we began to walk to a less intrusive area. "I am fine. How are you?"

He replied, "Listen you can't find me out here or in the book. (meaning the telephone book) I'm going to give you my number so you can call me. You are a graceful woman." He was implying, I could not find him because he is unreachable with his superstar status. I was talking to a superstar. Before I could reply a woman came from behind and as she walked by she pulled his coat tail firmly. It reminded me of when The Pastor pulls the bottom of the jacket of the preacher, when he is preaching too long. Gesturing your time is up! He gave her a look of irritation and a defined Shhh! Can't you see I am talking with someone?

The woman did not like the sense of him speaking with me. She was jealous. I looked and smiled and thought she has no reason to be jealous it was just a conversation. I warmly smiled, while attempting to make her feel at ease. I replied, "Well first I want to say I am honored and flattered of your interest but I am a Preacher and a Healing Minister." He looked at me with bewilderment. I explained, "I am a Healing Minister." (There were kids playing in wheelchairs in a distance; as most children love to sample the wheel chair.) While I pointed to the wheel chair I said, "Like people who are in the wheelchair right there. I tell them to get up and walk." Without any response and no emotion he turned around and just walked away. It was awkward. He just turned around and left. He didn't say thanks but no thanks, he didn't say well it was nice meeting you, see you around. He just simply turned around and walked away. As he walked in the distance he caught up with they woman who just kind of hung around while we were talking. They began arguing and walking. As they began to leave I thought to myself, I know her and she recently got married. I allowed my eyes to follow the coat sleeve of the red jacket she was wearing. I got to her left hand and I could see the gold wedding band she was wearing. I had seen her husband before in a picture and this man was not her husband. I awoke

Thus sayeth The Spirit. When the enemy of lust and perversion approaches, tell the enemy about me and he will either become quiet and flee or he will stay and listen for a littler while, but continue to talk about me and he will still flee. I want my people to know that the flashier the product is the less it represents me. Flash is only temporary and flash is only for pride. Flash gives the illusion of richness and favor but my graceful brings favor humility. Know the difference.

Bonus Round #2

Thus sayeth The Spirit of the True and Loving God. I am a consuming fire that can rage or put out the flames. I prefer to put out the flames. I love my children as the baby cub is loved by his mother. Love is a word that is used often out of context. To love me, means to have a heart and a desire for my souls; souls that belong to me, souls that go back to God. To love is to free yourself from all of the unwanted past failures. Are you loving your self today? Have you freed your mind from all of the guilt and pain? Jesus my son was freed from the snare of the pains of death and he took all your bondage to the cross with him. To love is to place that which is broken into the baggage of broken pieces. I am the sorter of the broken pieces. In my spirit you will find the items have been mended. Reach in the bag and pull out my glory. There is little time left to show my love and evangelize to the ones who are still searching for their pieces. Know the seasons of change. We are in a season where the ice crystals are changing into sun drops and the sun drops have emitted frost. The seasons have changed. Follow change and you will find my glory. We are in our last hours, days and minutes. The clock has struck twelve and the pumpkin is changing backwards into the mice. Bewildering, but we are in an opposite of time, for in the last days the seasons will change. Go back to the first love and you will find a season of stability in an unstable world.

THE BIG PARTY

DAY 11
Friday
January 31, 2014
THE BIG PARTY

I dreamed I went to a party. It was a big party. This was an annual party. It reminds me of the bible and where it talks in the Old Testament about the Year of Jubilee the celebration of being brought out of bondage. Leviticus 25, 27 (KJV). This is a celebration of liberty and because God's people were free they celebrated. In my dream the entire town participated in the celebration. There were a group of girls talking with this important man that invited them to celebrate in his suite. The suite reminded me of when you get tickets to see a NBA game and you are invited to celebrate in the private suites owned by dignitaries. His celebrity; status pad was in the high-rise standing next to us. They were talking to him on the phone, "We can't get up there!" Her voice carried from trying to talk over the large crowds around them. He must have asked, "Why not?" She replied, "Because we can't get past security."

I rode to the gathering with these girls talking to he man on the phone. My dream no longer took an interest with being with them. I left them as the police began to question and interrogate their presence at the building. I caught up with a different group of girls I knew. Tracy Montgomery gave me a tag along approval to hangout with her and her crew of friends attending the Jubilee. Tracy was a woman that allowed me the privilege of teaching a bible study at her home while church planting in my native city Lansing, Michigan. It was nice of her to open her home to receive the Word of God to her and her family. Here we were in my dream and this time Tracy opened her car to me. The bible declares when you receive a prophet you get a prophet's reward. Mathew 10:41. Tracy and I jumped out of the car as we made our way to the beach alongside of some beach-front properties. The city was celebrating in The Jubilee. We got out of her little burgundy bug car as we walked out of the parking structure. Tracy got ahead of me and I found myself side tracked with a group of men that were, maintenance persons for the villa-like beach front properties. One of the men pushed me too the ground between some cars. When he pushed me to the ground, I realized I was no longer myself but in actuality I was another woman. I was the woman that had been missing. God had given me the ability to feel like myself but really I was someone else. This is called Transfer of The Spirit. It was as if the real me was standing on the side and viewing the abduction of a real incident in the natural world. I was watching the missing woman being abducted. The man placed his foot on my back. My body was transferred and no longer was I black but I was this white girl wearing a white bikini laying face down praying someone would find me before the worst would happen. I feared the worst!

Tracy back tracks. "Has anyone seen my friend?" She inquired. She knew she had lost me in the height of the celebration. The man pressured the soul of his foot into by back. I knew he was saying, "If you make one sound I will crush all the bones in your back." I knew he would crush my chest. I sighed with a cry of terror. I began praying quietly. "Jesus please let them find me." Tracey gathered larger men, she knew. She prepped them saying, "We need to find my friend. I feel she may be in trouble. I was praying rather not me but the white woman I could see as I stood there on the side in a ghostly form looking. The man could hear her and the others looking for me. I guess the man got spooked and ran. The other men Tracy sent looking for me found me and took me to the jeep they owned that sat in the fresh sunshine. Tracey caught up with them. "We found here over her." They said. "She replied with, "Where is she?" "Over here" They said as they took her to me; me this white woman. We found her on the ground. She is bruised some but she is ok. They tried to abduct her. As I was reunited with Tracey I awoke.

Thus sayeth the Spirit of GOD, We are in a season where the abducted are not the real abducted but it is just a figment of our thought and imagination. They enemy comes to steal kill and destroy but I came that you may have life and have it more abundantly. If you feel out of body it means you are present with Christ, because to be present with Christ means you are in The Spirit and if you worship the true and living God you must do it with a humble heart and a pure spirit for I am looking for such to worship me. Gather the loins of your life as the woman gathered her composure and entered into a new area of sunshine. Gather you barns and cash them into the harvest of the ocean front for as the poor man seeks food so does the poor in spirit; food that will feed him for eternity a food where he never grows hungry; a food that is only found in me. How else did I feed the 5000 beside the natural food I gave them spiritual wisdom look between the pages of the lines of the book for your revelation. Step into a life of prayer and fasting as I will reunite you also with the lost you. My spirit has spoken. Step out of body and step into my glory, step into My Spirit.

Bonus Round #3

Thus sayeth GOD. We have gone through round 1 and 2 now we are in round 3. Round 3 is a round where the fighter gets accustomed to being in the ring. There are 12 rounds in the fight and in the 3rd round the fighter gets to know who his opponent is. Your opponent is in the round, in the ropes, in the square, the opponent is all around but who is wearing the gloves? You are. Most of the damage is done with the gloves. Look what's in your hands. The Sword of The Spirit; My Word will carry the battle because when we get to the twelfth round there is a title ship belt waiting that only can fit your mid -section because the top of you is waiting for the crown of glory. When the fighter is crowned he is crown with all glory and power for being a champion. There is champion inside of you. You have won the battle and gained the crown. You have won the battle and gained the title now it is time to check out of the ring and go into the final round this is the round of the knock out. Knock out the enemy with one punch knock the enemy out with me "The Blood". I hear the crowd roaring. I hear the angels applauding, for you have won. You have won because you have overcome the odds; a Christian in a cruel world; a Christian in a cruel ending; a Christian in a cool society. You are not of the world but in the world. A peculiar person you are called because your battle is not of this world but it is of My Kingdom. Get it! You are fighting for a kingdom you've never seen in a different world.... yes you get it. Keep fighting! Keep hoping! Keep dreaming because this battle is not yours but mine… It's The Lords.

R.E.S.P.E.C.T.

DAY 12
Saturday
February 1, 2014
R.E.S.P.E.C.T.

dreamed I lead a company. It was a large company. I dreamed the company was becoming successful. One day a trusted confidant came to see me and reported "The Spirit" of the employees. She said they were becoming disgruntled, complainers, mockers and scornful. I couldn't grasp why they felt this way because in my opinion everything was going well. So I thought. I treated them especially well. We gave them great compensation, bonuses and generous vacations. We treated them with value. I told her, "Ok". I formed a meeting to hear the voice of the people. We met in a storefront space located in the mall. The space was very large. There had to have been at minimum one thousand people falling in the doors. They were loud, dismayed, inattentive and rude. They entered and I could hardly start the meeting. This person needed to run out; to their car, to get this and another person, needed to go, get that. In and out the door they went and came back and forth. They were talking in an intrusive manner to the meeting. The annoyance of The Spirit of the people made me feel rejected and the meeting had not even started yet. They simply lacked R.E.S.P.E.C.T.

I started the meeting. I went to the podium and went right to the heart of the matter. I didn't start off with hello or thank you for coming. I said, "It has been called to my attention that a number of you are dissatisfied and I am here to hear the heart of you and see if I can bear your burdens with change." The floor was open. One said, "I don't like this….. And I don't like that….." In the dream I could not hear what they were saying. They were not really saying any complaints. I felt the "Spirit of Discord" in the people. Their hearts had been turned against the company without a valid reason. Then a woman spoke up, "I don't like the fact that Jesus is mentioned. I have my own religion and I don't want to be forced to accept or hear that." This was the only complaint I physically heard. I instantly knew that Satan had infiltrated the vineyard and was beginning to turn the people away from the infrastructure of the company. The leadership of the business was lovers of Christ and the employees did not have a valid reason to become heard in their hearts. I could feel my passion to take the floor now!

I stood with authority. I spoke with fervency and poise, "Well let me say this, this company was founded on morals, value and commitment. I Am A Preacher!" The people looked surprised as if they did not know. "This company stands on and will advance based on the very thing that started it. It will move forward in Jesus Christ and God! How many people left the old company I managed and came with me to start this new one? Raise your hands." Almost half of the people raised their hands. I knew if the "other hands" of the people left the company it would disassemble the operations. I went to say further with the conviction of a preacher, "So I know they will stay." The other company I managed closed down. I took the people that battled with me in the hard times of the old business. We went through the hardship of dissolving the company together. I took with me when we started the new company the employees that never left the old business and stood behind the leadership, and said "We are here with you until the end." I said it again, but this time I was I knew I was talking to somebody; and I said it with authority, "I know they will stay!" I was letting "The Devil" know, the demon of disassembly, the destroyer, "I Know They Will Stay" In a no weapon formed against us will prosper tone. "Now if the rest of you want to leave, Get!....Up!... Right!...Now! Walk out that door and I mean it. Because I know that the same God that made it possible for this to start, will build it back up and it will be better." I could see and feel better production, better customer service, better sales, healthier distribution, better planning and a stronger leadership. "If you must complain then you must go." I then awoke.

Thus sayeth the Spirit of GOD, "This dream is for those who are afraid to face the demands and pressures of the "Devil of Compromise". Compromise will create an environment for selling your soul; being sold out for what others are pressuring you to believe; a lie. Satan wants you to believe a lie, that if you choose his way it will give immediate gratification. The Demon of Compromise always but A.L.W.A.Y.S. chooses to infiltrate your house through the one he views as the weaker; the baby lamb; the baby that is spiritually a new birth. I have come that you may know the difference. I am writing these words that you may become spiritually strengthened. You become strengthened by manifesting the Fruit of The Spirit.

> Galatians 5:22-23 But the fruit of the Spirit is love, joy, peace, long-suffering, kindness, goodness, faithfulness, gentleness, self-control. Against such there is no law

The enemy is seeking whom he may devour. He seeks to devour all things that are built on The Rock; Christ my Son, business built on the rock, homes built on the rock, love built on the rock and finally prisons built on the rock. Well why do you say prisons? I am everywhere. I am in prisons also. I am a God that is omnipotent, omnipresence. My Spirit is everywhere! The enemy sends to prisons the lack of hope. You know Peter was in prison and I was there. I sent my cavalry to open the doors of murder and let out that which was to be slain. Stay focused! Don't loose hope and most of all don't lose to compromise. Selah"

The dream really felt real. The enemy was running a ribbon of discord through what God had built and with all the conviction of my life I knew God would come through for us again. I didn't mind letting the things go that seemed to keep it functional. God was showing that he keeps it functional, not man. So many times we believe in and depend on the skills of others to keep it together, not acknowledging that God not only keeps it together but he is the one that put it together. Trust in God not man and when we compromise this we are weakening the entourage. People can fail us but God will never fail us.

POT OF GOLD

VISION
February 1, 2014
POT OF GOLD

In the moment of my prayers, the Lord showed me a vision of a large pot. The type of pot was cast iron and large enough to hold at minimum, one ton of gold. The gold was melted and liquid. There was a hand with a rod stirring the gold and removing the impurities in the gold. Round and round the gold went in the pot. It began to form circular ripples in the pot. Then the pot then poured into a mold. The mold was of me, in a figured that stood 6feet tall. Once the mold of me was poured, then the pot began to pour molds of other people. One then two were poured until there were thousands of molds being poured. Then there were millions. They all then began to ascend into the heavens. They were being caught up like The Rapture envisions. God then spoke to me and said, "This is The Body of Christ walk streets of gold."

The Lord was very clear. "Walk streets of gold." He did not say "walking" but walk streets of gold. This vision is for today's believer. You are current in your walk on streets of gold right now. Why put off tomorrow for what needs to be done today. We are in a season of gold. Although the price of gold in this world is down the price of God's gold never changes. Gold is something that needs to be purified before it can enter into God's rest. The word of God says he tries us and once we are processed we come out as pure gold. 1 Peter 1:7(KJV) Only the pure in heart will see God. Mathew 5:8 (KJV). While we are here on earth God seeks to purify us. When he is finished making us a pure specimen we then walk his streets of gold in the spirit realm and in the natural sense. Which yellow brick road we follow is purely up to Christ himself. God's message with this vision is to stay on the gold yellow brick road. All roads lead to home. There will be many forks in the road meaning you will go many different journeys on these yellow brick roads but all roads lead to home. You can't walk on a gold path and not be golden. This is your golden moment! Take full charge and full speed. Grab hold of the reigns and don't look back. The journey is going to be long and sometimes tough but grab hold of the gold. God has placed all things under your feet, even gold.

SPECIAL RETREAT

DAY 14
Monday
February 3, 2014
SPECIAL RETREAT

I dreamed I went to an event that was a women's retreat, women's brunch or a special gathering for women. The event was centered on Christian Education. The people were educating themselves about The Holy Spirit in their lives. The special healing service took place in a banquet hall. During the service they served food and the preach spoke. During the event I sat at the table, closest to the wall, people used to travel to the powder room. During the height of the service, while some were experiencing Chara which is the Greek word for gladness (to experience Chara is the Holy Spirit's mighty rushing wind of gladness) The Holy Spirit said to me, "Get up and lay your hands on them." The Lord was referring to the people who were walking to the powder room and ones returning from the powder room. They reminded me of people on a flat escalator going back and forth during the event. I got up and began to pray for the people and laying my hands on them. The Holy Spirit was moving upon them. I was mostly speaking in tongues. Every person I laid my hands on was under demonic attachment. I could literally feel the dark presence on the people. I laid my hands on at least 20 people. I could feel the battle in the Spirit Realm.

I came upon a man and I began praying for him and laying my hands on him. While praying in tongues of The Spirit of the demonic presence on this man was much stronger than the others I had prayed for. The Holy Spirit said, "Tell it to come out." I said calmly and with authority, "Satan Come Out!" The man's face began to twist in disfigurement. The calm man I encountered a few minutes ago turned into a visual face full of hatred, malice, deception, murderous, rage, anger and perverseness all twisted into his face. His visage was marred. I had seen The Devil in his natural self. As Satan began to come out of the man he showed how he looked. I noticed in the dream the others I prayed for were demonically possessed also and I could feel the dark, satanic spirits in them but the spirits did not respond until I addressed it by name and commanded it to come out. I then awoke.

Thus sayeth The Spirit of The God of Life, "Satan is in The Church. His ways, His thoughts, His manipulation is amongst you. This is no secret, but what is a secret is out. It is known to you how to get rid of satanic covert operations in your lives in your homes, at your jobs and in our ministries. It is through prayer and commanding he comes out. Those three words in prayer will make change. Notice there was no change with the demons in the dream until the woman of God told it to come out. She spoke to The Spirit. As Peter said, not I but The Lord rebuke you. He spoke to the spirit. You must speak to the diseases in your life to come out. I have given you authority to trample on oppression. Take your authority. It is available.   Speak to your circumstance. Come Out! Speak to you afflictions, Come Out! Speak to the dark area! Come Out! I will deliver. I will deliver you from the dark moments I will deliver you from addictions to Drugs, Sex, Marijuana, Headaches, Cancer, Body Soul and Spirit Diseases. Just tell it to come out in my name, and we know anything we ask in my name, shall be given. I deliver All Demonic Activity when requested. Today is your day for Super Hyper Release."

HALF WAY THERE

DAY 14
Tuesday
February 4, 2014
HALF WAY THERE

I dreamed I was at a family cook out. The cookout was being held over to Leatha's mother's house. Leatha is a good friend of mine. We shared our young adult years together. Her mother Caroline has always been the type of mother that shared her home and love with the neighborhood young adults. She has always been nice. I went to her home for a cook out and they had great food on the menu. Caroline then suggested we go outside in the back yard to enjoy the rest of the cook out in the great weather. I thought it was a great idea. I love to be outside in GOD's nature. The back yard was really large. There had to have been at least an acre of back yard. We walked outside and then we crossed pass a sycamore tree. When we crossed the path of the tree, I looked down and there were hundreds and hundreds of serpents on the ground. She began walking on them. I could not believe my eyes. She said, 'Come on.' She acted as though it were something normal. I was apprehensive. I looked further and as she began to walk through the serpents I could see anacondas lying on the ground. They were large and long. I stood there and I said to myself "I am not going through there." I awoke.

Thus sayeth The Spirit of God, "We are in a place where the grass does grow and the grass was green but what the grass was holding was The Spirit of The Enemy. You are in a place where there are the mature Christian; as what the mother represented. The mature matriarch has the ability to walk around the midst of the strategies of the enemy. The matriarch has the power to subdue kingdoms. The matriarch has the knowledge to take it to The Lord in prayer. She does not break, buckle or give in. She is tall and graceful. She is graceful in my words. She knows which scripture to apply to the right situation she is An Apostle. She takes the kingdom of God by force. She is tall and rich. She knows how to work the power that is within her. She doesn't back down. The smaller person which was the author of the book she represented the Christian who still lacks food but drinks milk. She has apprehensiveness. She walks away in the face of danger. She does not hold steady to my word. She wavers. She allows others to make her decisions. She has not fully decided on me and she has nothing to stand on. The younger woman represented the immaturity of the immature saint; the saint who causes havoc in the doors of the church, the saint who constantly pressures The Pastor to hold her hand in love; The Pastor who has not a readily available commitment to her. She is the saint who said I do with her lips but her actions say differently. She is the saint that refuses to grow. She is the saint that has an ego. She is the saint that must get it right. She is the saint that is up all night. She is the saint that takes pills. She is the saint that wants to kill. She is the saint that must come back. She is the saint I want to deliver. She is the saint that has the river, the river of afflictions. She is the saint I am calling to come closer. She is the saint I want to carry through the serpents den. She is the saint where we always have to do it again. She is the saint I am calling to me. She is the saint within me. She is the saint I'm giving another chance. She is the saint that's tired of the dance. She is the saint in you. Does this apply to you?"

THE PINK PASS

DAY 15
Wednesday
February 5, 2014
THE PINK PASS

I dreamed I was at work and overheard a conversation. The person on the phone said, "Well you've got to give her more severance pay than that. This is all you're going to give her? Well we will have to tell her today." I heard another voice say, "Yes we will have to tell her. This is awful. How will we move forward? Oh my!" The other voice said, "Well I'm so sorry. We will let her know." They hung up the phone. I knew they were talking about me. I was going to be fired from my job. I then awoke.

Thus sayeth The Holy Spirit. "Pink slips come in many different colors but they carry the same message; termination. To be terminated from your employer means that I have freed up your time for my glory. I have freed your mind for my service. I laid-off The Leviticus Tribe from working for the Israelites, and from debt. I freed them that they could minister to me. When I take away, I am a restorer. If you have lost your work or way; look to me to restore. The God of Restoration Selah"

When I lost my source of income due to the Automotive Collapse of 2008; I was unable to pay my mortgage. I lived in my house for years without the ability to pay. I guess when my file got to the top of the foreclosure files God allowed someone to drop the file. God spoke to me one day, "Pack your house up because you are moving and this time next year you will not be living in this house, but a better house." I packed the entire house with anticipation of moving. I lived out of boxes for about 11 months. I can remember murmuring and complaining to myself about having to "live out of boxes.' I liked being able to go to a drawer and pick out what I needed. I resented having to dig in boxes for the right pair of shoes. I forgot half the things I owned. I owned so much. I was being conditioned by God to see, I really didn't need a whole lot to live. I was complaining and out of nowhere I heard the Holy Spirit say, "You could be living out of boxes outside." With a "we can make that happen tone." It was winter time in Michigan and it gets really cold in The Northern United States. The message was so clear and convicting of my heart. It felt a piercing. I was shocked God spoke in this manner and then fear and trembling came over me. I fell to my knees and told God how sorry I was. I knew he was the only one keeping me from being on the street and here I was complaining. That spring God opened the door for me to plant a church 100 miles from my home. I signed a lease for a 9000sft building. It was a warehouse. When we got the building it was close to demolition. It was rough but God allowed me to see the potential. We began painting and building the sanctuary and pulpit. GOD sent us the resources for all this work to be accomplished. The Holy Spirit said, "I want the 1st service held in 2 months." We raced to get the first Dedication Service started on time. Everything happened so fast. I did not anticipate everything to move so swiftly. When God moves he moves. I was so busy I never had time to go back to my house. I was preaching every Sunday and being a pastor to the people. I met with people almost daily who needed prayer. Some were on the brink of destruction. I was teaching Bible Study every Wednesday. I held Friday Night Prayer Service and a daily 5am Teleconference Prayer Line for the church. I had to find the time to oversee the church's mechanic repair shop. It was chaotic and hectic. My car broke down with a cracked head gasket which is usually costly to fix. I could only drive one mile and the car would start overheating. I could not travel back home 100 miles away. On top of all that I was a single mother with two children. I was staying with my mother and The Holy Spirit said, "I want you to move into the church." I finally went home with a truck and only had time to gather my bed and a few things. I moved in the church. I realized one night wow, I don't live in that house but I live in God's house and yes it is much better; A Church. God is surprisingly funny I thought. My time was freed so I could serve God.

I finally found time to go home. I had plans to move my things but with little money and time, it was nearly impossible during this season in my ministry. The Holy Spirit spoke to me with clarity right before I arrived home, "Regardless to what you find or don't find; I am with you." When I arrived I found my home entirely emptied with a lock box on the door. The house was a beautiful 4000 sft, home with two stories, cathedral ceilings, three bedrooms, two kitchens, two living sitting rooms and two full bathrooms. It was beautiful because it was mine. There is nothing like having your own space. The neighborhood was quiet and child friendly. All my personal items, washer and dryer, expensive furniture sets, dining room furniture, bed room sets, heirloom furniture, kitchen table chairs, two 62' flat screen television(s), diamonds, mink coats, fox coats, mink hats, patio furniture and pictures was gone. I lost everything. My heart sank. I was instantly reminded of:

Mathew 19:29 And every one that hath forsaken houses, or brethren, or sisters, or father, or mother, or wife, or children, or lands, for my name's sake, shall receive an hundredfold, and shall inherit everlasting life. (KJV)

When we chose to follow Christ we must be willing to risk it all. Risk fame and fortune, risk highs and risk our own lives. Christ is looking for us that are willing to be martyrs for his kingdom. We were created for his glory and to worship him. I kept it a secret that I lost my home and everything inside. I lost everything it took me so long to work for and acquire. I worked so hard for years I was a hard working woman. I told no one. I got back to the church and I preached and pastored as usual. A member of our church Patrick bought a new car. Then a few weeks later he and his wife bought another new car. They brought both the cars to the church and said, "We bought the first car but we don't like it because it's a stick shift. We want you to have it. They put they keys in my hand and said here. God Bless You!" They went on to say, "Don't worry about the first two car payments because we have paid them ahead including the insurance." I drove it that day. I gave my broken car away for free to a man with mechanical skills that could fix cars. The story gets better. Here comes the glory. Forty-five days prior, I was walking down the sanctuary's main aisle to my bedroom and the Holy Spirit said, "I love you Nikki with an unspeakable love and in less than thirty days you will see a new car." I didn't tell anyone what The Holy Spirit spoke to me. I wrote it down with the date in my journal. I was led by God to show what I had written to my step-father Tom. I remember clearly when he read the journal entry. He smiled softly. You know that smile a person gives that says; I would like to see this happen with my own eyes." When that new car was delivered to me my stepfather was standing there and in shock. He just stared at the floor.

"He said, "I will pay the car notes and insurance. Every month he was faithful with his tithes. He used his tithes to pay the car note and insurance which happened to be 10% of his first fruits. The story gets better. A few months later I traveled to Tennessee to help plant a church. When I came back home and a member of the church had a house and the bank had cleared the title for no reason. I could remember praying with that person for the home a couple years prior. They walked up to me gave me the keys and said we want to donate the house as a parsonage for the church. I moved in after a few minor cosmetic changes. People just gave me furniture. They responded, "Oh you're moving into a house? I want to give this to you. Sofas dishes, pots pans, new washers and dryers were delivered. One day my sister appeared with boxes and garbage bags of new clothes. She said, "The Lord told me to give these to you. I don't know why but here take these clothes. They are so nice." She came every day for an entire week delivering more and more clothes to the church. It has been two years later and she still brings me new clothes and coats. I never told her about losing my house and clothing. This reminds me of how God did not allow the Children of Israel to lack clothing or shoes for forty years and nothing they wore was old or torn.

Deuteronomy 29:5 And I have led you forty years in the wilderness: your clothes are not waxen old upon you, and thy shoe is not waxen old upon thy foot. (KJV)

God will restore. He is a God of restoration. Look to the hills from which cometh your help. Your help comes from the Lord. God judges us on our diligence and he promises to help us when we turn to his ways. He is a rewards those who diligently seek him.

GRAND MOTHER

DAY 17
Friday
February 7, 2014
GRAND MOTHER

I dreamed about my grandmother Lucille. Bless her soul. She passed in 2003 at the age of 99. She was three weeks shy of turning 100. I dreamed she was terminally ill. Remembering my grandmother is a memory of a saint. She read her bible more than anyone I know. She believed in Christ and her soul was anchored in the Lord.

I dreamed while she was ill, my mother Barbara was distraught about my grandmother being ill. Do you remember Barbara? She was the woman with the nails in her hands. The same person with so much confidence in her dream was distraught in this dream. In my dream, I was lying on the couch asleep and dreaming. My mom said, "I'm going to the store." I replied, "Ok." In the dream I felt like I was the supporter. You know the person that holds the family together. Just as I was awaking from my nap my Mom came in the door. She had a look in her eyes of despair. "Mama's gone." She said as she sobbed lightly. My mother was at peace with the passing of Grandma. "I replied intensely, "Why didn't you tell me." I questioned her with concern. "Well you were asleep and I didn't want to wake you." said Barbara My Mother.

I thought to myself why wouldn't you want to wake me for news like that? We were at the repass and I wanted to take my top layer coat off. It was very warm in the room. I took my coat off and there was a mirror. I looked in the mirror and on the side of my dress were openings. The dress was made in this fashion with openings on the sides. I felt very uncomfortable with the openings showing. I thought they were too revealing. I placed my jacket back on. The waiter brought the salads to the tables. The repass was full with people. I sat at the table with my friends. Some one said, "Isn't that your father?" My biological father's name is Albert. I love my father. In the dream my father walked up to me with a flattering smile. He was dressed very sharply. He wore a coral blue with navy blue casts blazer. The style of the blazer had puffed shoulders (leg-of-mutton style) and a tapered waist line. He had a red handkerchief in the breast pocket. His shoes were white with red wing tips. He was so fashionably dressed. I stood and said, "Hi Dad give me a hug." He replied and smiled, "Are you sure? Tom may get upset. He smiled in a mocking tone.

Thus sayeth the Spirit of GOD, "The red shoes are shoes that represent my spirit although we walk in the shoes of people we admire walking in my spirit is far more rewarding than walking in the shoes of a man that will burn over time. Burning shoes are shoes that cause the flame to run out. Christ wore shoes of fire. Fire in the shoes represent My Spirit at work; working in the believer's heart. The blue jacket represents the blues of the person on the out side but, the heart is merry of the inside. The inside of the heart is where I place my judgment. Every man will be judged according to that which worked in his heart. The picture of the father was not out of character as her father has always been a classy act, but there comes a time in the believer's life when the class act must meet the white board. White boards are erasable. The scars of hurt are not erasable only healable. The smart-aleck connotation represent the slyness of the heart that wants to say I love you and you know I have always been there for you; I just didn't not know how to show you. Come to a spiritual father who is there. Knows how to show and is manifested with results. Relationships are a hard thing to conquer. This is why my son conquered your relationship with me at the cross. This is the complexity of the father son; father daughter relationship. There is healing available for every bruised and broken spiritual relationship in the book of the pages of My Chapter reads Romans. Many are the afflictions of the righteous but the Lord delivers them all. Be ye healed in My Name this is a psalm of healing. Healing is where the blood forms clots and carries antibodies to the wounded center and the antibodies carry cells and the cells carry the nucleus. Come into the nucleus where there is healing come in to me. The God that healeth all. Jehovah Rapha the God that healeth thee. Selah

I Was Walking And Went To Bend Over And The Holy Spirit Said, "I Am Doubling You Dreams. Instead Of One Dream A Night There Will Be Two And I Am Shortening The Length Of 30 Days."

CHARLIE

DAY 18
Sunday
February 9, 2014
CHARLIE

I dreamed I was at war. The warring spirits name was Charlie. I owned a house and in this house were my daughter Kennedy the 4yr old and another woman named Tina. Tina is a young lady I met while working in Detroit, Michigan. She was a nice young girl. I always admired her. She had tenacity. She managed her home with four children and a husband. She found the strength to come to her job every day. I loved to see her so ambitious. In my dream she was in this house with me. The house was a large historical southern style small mansion.

A man came in the house through the front door. He wore a black all weather over coat. He had black hair. He was medium built. He was a white man with olive toned skin. He could have possibly been Italian or Grecian. I quietly ran crouched down to prevent him from seeing me. I whispered, "Tina! Tina!" I could not get her attention without being exposed. I ran upstairs. I knew if I made it up the stairs I could run outside through the upstairs back door leading to the porch. The house was unusual. There was a back porch on the 2nd floor and there were grandeur style stairs that lead from the back porch to the sidewalk. The house was obviously built on a hill.

By the time I made it up the stairs and to the back porch; Charlie had mysteriously arrived to meet me there. I say mysteriously because he did not have the time to make it there, where I made it; he had to travel further to get there. He was so fast. I should have won, but I didn't and I was there faced with a confrontation with Charlie. I turned around and began to run. I ran back down the hallway, I came up. As I ran there was a door in front of me. The door surprisingly was not there going up but coming down was a heavy brown door with historical dead bolt style locks. There were at least two locks on the door. The door was open and I ran through the door. I closed the door and tried to lock it so Charlie could not get through but I could not work the lock. Charlie was so close. By this time Tina was behind me. She was frightened but she put me in the mind of an encourager. She was coaching me on how to work the lock. She said, "She doesn't know how to work the locks. She has never used these kinds of locks before. She can't get it." I decided not to continue trying to lock the door for fear I would be captured by Charlie. As Tina and I ran there was another door we had to go through. There was a lock on this door also. I couldn't lock it either. I was trying to lock Charlie on the other side but was unsuccessful. I went through three attempts and three doors but was unsuccessful. Charlie had captured me. I fought Charlie but Tina did not. She succumbed because of fear.

Charlie led us to the front of the house. When we got there others had joined Charlie. He had an operation. I could see one Spirit working on the computer and another Spirit working in the distance. Tina sat with those that ran Charlie's operation. The Spirits said, "It's not that bad being captured." They were physically and spiritually dead and didn't even know it. They were simply people who had been captured and conformed out of fear. I thought to my self, "I'm ESCAPING! Charlie is going to kill me anyhow." Charlie was a serial killer. Charlie was going to torture me because I was a runner. He came towards me as I tried to escape.

Charlie had these pencils and he was trying to drive them into my nostrils. I was fighting back. As the boxer drills the rhythm bags, this is what I was doing with Charlie as he attempted to drive the pencils into my nose. He said, "Whatever you do I am going to win." I struggled with Charlie and I made it out! As I escaped, I ran down the stairs of the front of the house. The front stairs were made in the same style as the back porch stairs. On my way down there was a woman coming down a set of stairs from the house next door. I told her to call the police. There was a man up there killing people. I warned her. I felt something hanging from my nose. I pulled it out. Charlie had won by driving those pencils into my nostrils. I did not know it. I was unaware. As I began to pull out the pencils I got light headed. If I had just left them in I wouldn't have lost so much blood. I began passing out but I had made it. I escaped. I was bruised and fighting for my life but there was still hope. I had to face fear and opposition but I refused to lose to Charlie.

Thus sayeth The Lord, "The runner in this revelation has run the race. They have kept the faith. To be crowned with a robe of righteousness is a spectacular event. Don't run from the war on terrorism. Charlie is the terrorist that enters the homes of my children. He tries to capture them with silly ladens. Charlie is a serial killer because he needs more coverts to run his principalities. You fight him not with your flesh but you fight him with my spirit. I am the capturer of Charlie. I have the ball and chain to compress him to torture my servants no more. Draw close to me. I give rest. I ease the weary soul. Come to me I heal the aching mind. You war not after the flesh but the spirit is in a war with Charlie. I ease the spirit of tiredness of Charlie. In a Charlie; the mind says yes Lord, but The Soul says maybe this time and then The Spirit says; I'm tired, this why I must strengthen your inner man daily. It's what I did for Paul. There is a winner in you. You may come out with battle scars but you win the battle because I fight for you. Come out of the snare of Charlie. Walk through the doors of escape, The Father, The Son and The Holy Spirit. I shut the door no man can close. I close the door on Charlie; the door of the warring spirit, the war of terrorism. Come out of captivity. Come to me. I am your savior. I save that which is lost. I save that which can't be found. I save souls. God"

Definition of Terrorism (The definition of Charlie)

n. **THE SYSTEMATIC USE OF TERROR** (The American Dictionary, Houghton Mifflin 1982)

In my dream Charlie was not one but many. The Spirit told Jesus when confronted, "My name is Legion for we are many." Mark 5:9. Legion represents and army of 6000 soldiers. Charlie had specific strategic spirits operating his mission. His mission is to steal kill and destroy God's people. I once warred with Charlie before I chose Christ. Charlie drains you until you have no life left. You either suffer or choose Christ. The others had made their choice in the dream. They were dead spirits because they did not choose life. Jesus told us to chose life and live.

John 11:25 Jesus said unto her, I am the resurrection, and the life: he that believeth in me, though he were dead, yet shall he live: (KJV)

Charlie chooses a systematical approach with the things of the world such as lusts to capture his spirits. Charlie appears to win but when we choose Christ we ultimately have won. We won a Crown.

THE HEIST

DAY 19
Tuesday
February 11, 2014
THE HEIST

On this night I dreamed, I owned a community house. The house was like an open apartment building with private rooms. The room doors were open and similar to a boarding house. I lived in the house and I owned and ran the house. There were also a lot of people living with me in my house and it had become a boarding home.

The people did not have a place to stay so they stayed there with me. I walked through the main hallway and I looked at the different scene of people in their rooms and I said to my self in an irritating tone, "I can't believe all these people live with me." In approval of my good works I then sighed and said, "Well I guess. I am doing it for the Lord." It reminded me of how the Lord desires we take others in and allow them to live with us with out charging them.

> Leviticus 25:35-36 And if thy brother be waxen poor, and fallen in decay with thee; then thou shalt relieve him: yea, though he be a stranger, or a sojourner; that he may live with thee. Take thou no usury of him, or increase: but fear thy GOD; that thy brother may live with thee. (KJV)

I walked by the room of young boys. They were seven and eight years old. There were about three boys. I had taken them in because they were without parents and homeless. Everyone that lived in the house was there because they were rejected by someone, either family, peers or society. The boys called me into their room. They shared a very large room. I went in and they said, "Do you want to buy any of this?" There were clothes lying on the beds; piles and piles of brand new clothes. There were brand new shoes in the boxes. They had everything everywhere as though they had been on a shopping spree. I said, "NO!" I began to question them, "Where did you get this stuff from?" I knew the stuff was stolen. Some of the stuff was still hanging out of the booster's bag. I knew they had taken this because they were too young to acquire these things with money and they were adult clothing. They were only seven years old. I said, "You guys stole these things. Why would you do this?" I walked out of the room after chastising them about what they were doing was wrong. I rubbed my temple on the way out in a tone saying, "This is too much right now. I will have to deal with them later." I walked into the next room. Omar was sitting on the bed. Omar is my niece Cabria's son's father. Omar was talking on the phone to Cabria. He was sad. He asked me, "When is my birthday?" I replied, "August 12." I noticed in his hand was a letter. He looked at the letter and said, "Yes it is right." (Referring to the birthday dates on the letter).

I had a look on my face that said, "What's wrong?" He told my niece Cabria, "I'm sorry but the paper says for me to report to the immigration deportation before my birthday August 12." This date was only a couple months away. He was being deported back to Pakistan his native country. I thought, "Oh No!" in despair. He was my nephew's father. He was a part of our family and we didn't want to loose him. He said with tears, "I don't know what happened. There must have been a hearing date and I missed it."

I said, "Well, we can get a lawyer." But we all knew that all hope was lost because at that stage he still had to leave when the lawyer worked on the case. In my dream that was the law and the law took precedence. There was no deviation from the law. He had to go through deportation. He had to leave the U.S.A.

Thus sayeth the Spirit of the Only True and Living God Jehovah, "As the mail is opened and the letter reads so does My Spirit speak. The house represents the Body of Christ because we are all one house; housing one Spirit. There are some in the house who have yet to be found. Seeking that which is lost means to get to the heart of their troubles. There are some in the house that are facing deportation. They will travel to a land that is barren. They will go to a land that has no hope for renewal they will go to a land that has no life. They will go to hell. A hell where there is no relief only gnashing of teeth. Deportation is real if you miss the letter. Paul wrote letters so did Peter, James and Isaiah, This is the call of true repentance. You have the thief in my house; The Body of Christ. Children who are young and don't know the way, have stolen their way in through the wrong sheep fold. They are in my heart; this is why I allow them to stay. But they are in violation of the law. No man may come to me except through The Son.

John 14:6 Jesus saith unto him, I am the way, the truth, and the life: no man cometh unto the Father, but by me.

My mercy has allowed this. You are tenders of my house. Find that which is lost in my house. They have no rest and show them the true way. Find Salvation and you will fine home.

Selah

Batty

DAY 20
Thursday
February 13, 2014
BATTY

I dreamed I was in a basement. The basement was a finished basement with bedrooms, living room and laundry area. There was a fluttering sound coming from the laundry room. I said something is in there. I thought maybe it was an animal that crept into the house. I sent a man to check it out. They came back and said, "It is a bat in there." I thought, "No way! How are we ever going to get a bat out of here?" I had to see for myself because I couldn't believe what they were saying. I braced myself. I went in there and I could not see the bat because it was dark. I saw a pair of eyes shining bright in the dark air. Yes it was a bat. The eyes represented eyes that could see very clearly. The eyes knew you were there and it was as if the bat was fearful of his surrounding and our presence. The bat could see us and we could obviously see him but his eyes were peculiar. They dominated his body and were round as marbles, dark brown with a medium brown ring around the outer eye. I didn't see the bats body, only his eyes. His body was hid due to the darkness of the room. I awoke

Thus sayeth GOD, "Bats are creatures I created to fly long distances in the night. The bat helps to prepare the air for the birds. They are on different time schedules to adapt to the surrounding in their adaptation. The bat is a creature that posses extreme precise fundamental senses. Although the bat can not see, his senses guide the way. Although you truly can not see your way my senses provide shelter, intuition and guidance for you just like the bat. You can't see my body but you have my eyes. Use my spiritual eyes I have given you to see into dark areas of your life. If you follow the bat you will know that at the end of his shift he searches for cover. Some go into mountains others into volcanoes some go into trees and other go in holes under ground. The under ground bat looks for food in burrows. I am petitioning you to search for your batty eyes. Batty comes from the acronym batasous. Batasous is a Greek synonym for look. The bat cannot see but he knows my voice. He knows the sound of the shofar. He knows the sound of the horn as Joshua and Caleb blew the horn for the walls to come down, so will you blow the sound and I will come down and remove your wall. I will step off my thrown if you blow hard enough with your spirit. Yes your spirit blows a sound. Your spirit travails for me. Your spirit laments for me. Your spirit waits for me to come to your rescue, so use your eyes to see the dark and use your eyes to see the light and know the difference."

Seashore

DAY 24
Thursday
February 13, 2014
SEASHORE

My dream took place in a town that sat on an ocean or sea side. There was constant precipitation in the air. You could smell the sea outside your door. My family and I went to the marketplace. This market place was very open. It was full of tourist, vendors and locals. It was very live and festive.

My brother George, stepfather Tom and my Mother all decided to rent a movie. In this seafront you could rent movies and bring your movie to movie stations. The stations were sit down areas with private screens. The screens were the size of flat screen computer monitors. The stations were similar to drive-in movie theaters but the screens were much smaller and the sitting areas were more intimate and you didn't need cars. There was moisture in the air and my brother's movie was less interesting than the movies we rented but somehow his movie was playing. We were not Sci-Fi fanatics so we didn't take an interest. I started a conversation with My Mother. We were standing and I began telling her about this dream I had the night prior. I said, "Mom, you know I had this really weird dream."

She replied, "Oh yea, what was it about?" I said, "I dreamed I was being vacuumed in by this enormous tornado. The tornado was different. The mouth of the tornado began forming in the middle of the sky but never touched the ground. It stayed in the sky. The opening was the size of a football field. It was dark grey on the outer and light grey inside. There was lightening throughout the tornadoes outer core. It was full of energy. The core of the tornado was calm and inviting. It was pulling my spirit towards it. I could hear God from inside the mouth saying, "Come to Me." The voice was very distinct. I was frightened until I heard the calm distinct voice. It was something else." She replied, "Oh really. Where were you?" I said, "I was standing in front of my boat house."

I lived in a house that sat right on the harbor dock. There were rows of houses made to float in the water. The outside market was a block away from my house. As we departed the conversation of the monster tornado, my father was ready to leave the market. He was waiting for the good part of the movie to come but it never came. They began to pack up. As we prepared to leave the sky became aggressive. The air began moving angrily in the sky. The clouds became instantly dark.

Pandemonium set in the people. Everything happened so fast. The clouds started taking form and shape into a tornado. The tornado began to form itself into the tornado that was in my dream. It looked exactly like it. I just told my mother minutes ago about the dream and now it was happening. It was simply unbelievable! Everyone started screaming and running. I got separated from my family in the midst of the pandemonium. I ran to my boat house. My plan was to get my car keys. Get in my car and drive away. The tornado was formed in a matter of seconds. I got inside the house and the lights went out. Everything was pitch-black. I was blind. I couldn't see. I could feel, so I felt along the walls until I got to the kitchen. The kitchen was only steps away. Everything in the house was only steps away. The house was very small and the kitchen was open and very tiny, it was a boat home. I kept my car keys in the kitchen on the counter. I was feeling my way. I found the keys! I opened the front door and the entire city was black. The storm had left and the tornado had left and the excitement was over. Just like that the massive tornado was gone. I kept dreaming but I can't share the rest of the dream because the Holy Spirit has spoken this to you and the rest is for me.

Thus sayeth God, I am the twister. I am The Euroclydon. I am the friendly weather friend. I am the source of all energy! I Am The Am That I Am. I am The God of Shadrach, Meshach and Abednego. I am The God of all existence. I am The God that can change you storms to fair weather. I am The God that ceases all storms. I am The God you choose to depend on. The storms of your life are there to run you to me right into the center of my joy. I sent the storm to send the rain. I sent the rain to send the trees. I send the trees to send you oxygen. What appears to be devastating is there to bring the H2O. It is there to bring you out. Concentrate on what the middle of the storm is saying. Come close to me while in the Cyclodone. When you come close the storm will pass. This is the revelation to making the storm disappear. This is the secret to make it go away. Draw close to me and what use to bother you will disappear. Selah

The Woman

DAY 27
Sunday
February 16, 2014
THE WOMAN

I dreamed I was visiting a woman. She was possibly an aunt. It was winter time and very cold. The heat went out at her house. She came out with an announcement before the house became unbearable. "We had my husband and I….had a few shut off notices and got a little behind. As a result they shut the heat off." She was very apologetic in her announcement. One person that was visiting them also became condemning. "That is a shame. I'm leaving. How can you have these people here with no heat?" They stated. I spoke, "Well it is ok. These things happen and it's just unfortunate. We will figure it out together." I wanted to stay and suffer in the cold with them. I knew I couldn't because I had two children. I then awoke.

Thus sayeth the Spirit. Heat is a result of fire. When the fire is out there is no heat left. Heat allows us to live in comfortable environments; but what about those who have no heat. They have lost their fire. They have lost their drive. They have dried out and dried up. All sources are dissipated. What about those with no fire that have, only you to depend on. Others have scorned them, mocked then, scandalized them and ran them through spiritual clamps; clamps that are placed on clothes, before they go through the wringer. People who condemn the misfortunes of others because they have used all their comforts and look to the comforts of others also; the greedy and non- caring. What about those who have no one to turn to but you; the man on the street corner; the woman with nothing to eat. I hear the comments of the scornful they say, "That is a shame." But what about them? They are hiders. They hid behind the scorns and their hearts are far from me. What about the homeless. What about Miriam? Aaron pleaded, Moses pleaded for her return. She was an outcast because of a mistake. And what about you? How can you intercede for the homeless? How can you help? How can you judge? How can you know to do right unless you help your neighbor? Help is a four letter word that says love. Help is a four letter word that says give. Help is a four letter word that says judge. Judge not or you will be judged. Give not and you won't have. Love not and you will not be loved. Care not and I will not care for you. I am observing the homeless and I am observing you. My spirit has spoken.

Definition of Scorn
1. Extreme contempt; that disdain which springs from a person's opinion of the meanness of an object, and a consciousness or belief of his own superiority or worth. Merriam-Webster Internet 2014
2. Contempt; or disdain felt toward an object or person considered despicable or inferior The American Heritage Dictionary 1982

COMPULSIVE CHRONIC DISORDER

DAY 28
Monday
February 17, 2014
COMPULSIVE CHRONIC DISORDER

I dreamed I was in the process of planning for outside street revivals. Four streets were my target for four Fridays. In reality I regularly minister Friday Night Healing revivals at various locations, but in my dream these locations were outside. They were block revivals. I chose the roughest blocks to minister on. I was in the process of calling the city to find out what I needed to close off certain streets. I went into a home of a young woman and her sister. One sister was likely in her late 30's she was a full figured woman. The young sister had a problem and the older sister was trying to mentor her about the problem. I did not know the women intimately. I don't even know how I got in their kitchen with them but I was there. They welcomed me as though they were familiar with me. The younger sister with the problem was very slender. She didn't look to be in the best health. Her face looked tired and her body looked starved. She was tall. She looked as though life was getting the best of her at such a young age. Neither of them had names in the dream so the Holy Spirit has told me to call them "Nameless".

The full figured woman Nameless said, "You do have a problem." The malnutrition Nameless replied. "I don't have a problem I just work a lot and take care of my kids. It is stressful. I just need to unwind sometime." The older Nameless replied with disparity and exhaustion, "You do it everyday. You have a problem." I firmly interjected, "Let me say this." They both gave me their attention with the respect a Pastor receives when they speak. I told Nameless with the Children, "You do have a Problem. You drink everyday. You drink a pint of liquor daily. Drinking of any type of liquor daily is a problem. You have a drinking problem and you are in DENIAL!" I was very straightforward. Nameless had no choice but to deal with what was being said about her by her sister and a Pastor. She became agitated saying. "Don't nobody know what I go through!" I responded to her, "Regardless to what you say. You have a problem called alcoholism." After hearing her excuses as to why she drinks and her denials I said, "I understand how you feel and what triggers your drinking. I lived with my husband for years; who was an alcoholic. He drank fifths of liquor over long periods and had a daily assignment to do it all day every day. My question to you (I asked bluntly), Do you want help? She said, "Yes." and agreed to receive help. She began to complain about the help, "I'm not going to Grand Rapids. It's too far.' Grand Rapids is a centralized city in the State of Michigan.

Most addicts don't want to conform to anything that requires effort because effortlessness is what got them on substances. I said, "Ok I will find something for you." She stated loudly as I was leaving, "And I don't want any place where I will have to spend the night."

I looked into rehabs and I found one she had previously visited. They brought up her file. "They administrator said, "She will need to stay here because she has been here seven times already." She has Compulsive Chronic Disorder. As I stood there, I was surprised. How could a person fail a program seven times and say, "They don't have a problem." I awoke.

Thus sayeth the Holy Ghost. Problems are tricky. Problems are situations we don't have the power, sustenance or ability to fix. A problem is an adverse affect of a choice or decision. A problem is adherent when you place your heart on others and me; Gods Spirit. There are many problems but only one solution.

When you allow me to solve your problems you never revisit them again in this life. I am the true and only problem solver. The rest are problem dealers. They deal with the obstruction. I handle the obstruction. I am not only the problem solver but I mend all things back to their original habitat. The persons remained Nameless because I want you to place a name there you see with these problems and you can know realistically the problem they truly have. I then want you to tell them about me every chance you have. Simply tell them about Jesus, the heart fixer, the problem solver and The Lover. I will reward you for words spoken. I will reward you for the effort given. I will reward you for a life you saved. Jesus

POURED OUT AND NOT POURED INTO VISION

February 18, 2014

In Conclusion I had a vision of a coffee pot with water being poured into the coffee pot. The Lord began to minister to me, he said, "We are made into a new pot of coffee. We are made anew to come out now as Christ.

1. We are poured out like an old pot of coffee is poured out.
2. We are rinsed clean by Jesus like you would rinse the emptied stale coffee pot.
3. We are filled back up with the Holy Spirit, like you would fill the fresh clean coffee pot back up with fresh water.
4. Then we are poured into GOD like the fresh water is poured into the percolator for brewing.

The body of Christ has it backwards. Most think GOD is poured into us but we are truly poured into him. Every day is a fresh day. Everyday is a new day to be emptied out, rinsed fresh, filled up and poured into God's Kingdom to do kingdom work.

Mathew 9:38 "Pray ye therefore the Lord of the harvest, that he will send forth labourers into his harvest." (KJV)

God is seeking fresh laborers. If your assignment is being delayed God is waiting for you to empty yourself out, to become a fresh beam of light pouring into the souls of the lost. This book is a book that depicts the believers and non followers of Christ. It shows how the lost are seeking to be found and delivered. God calls us to take the office of an evangelist, 2 Timothy 4:5; within that office is the assignment of searching for those in need of help. I am writing you to encourage you to find the lost, seek them out, minister to them, love them and tell them about the love of Jesus Christ.

About the Author

Allyssa Narvaez is a world renowned Minister of Faith Healing. Her ministry is heard throughout the world with life changing testimonies of healing and deliverance. The healing ministry of Jesus Christ can be felt by the masses for God's glory through Allyssa. Allyssa's ministry reach extends beyond social media, internet & radio broadcast to the readers and hearts of those willing to believe in the supernatural ministry of The Holy Spirit. As a called five-fold Prophet, Teacher, Pastor, Evangelist, and Apostle she enjoys the calling of Church Planting. She has built multiple businesses and churches for the glory and admonition of God. Continue to stay in-touch with Allyssa Narvaez.

STAY CONNECTED

WWW.ALLYSSANARVAEZ.COM

WWW.HEALEDINJESUSNAME.COM

FACEBOOK/PROPHETESS ALLYSSA NARVAEZ

TWITTER/ ALLYSSANARVAEZ

www.ingramcontent.com/pod-product-compliance
Lightning Source LLC
LaVergne TN
LVHW021543080426
835509LV00019B/2815